W9-AEE-333

SPORTS HEROES AND LEGENDS

Derek Jeter

Read all of the books in this exciting, action-packed biography series!

Hank Aaron

Barry Bonds

Joe DiMaggio

Tim Duncan

Dale Earnhardt Jr.

Lou Gehrig

Mia Hamm

Tony Hawk

Derek Jeter

Michael Jordan

Michelle Kwan

Mickey Mantle

Shaquille O'Neal

Jesse Owens

Jackie Robinson

Babe Ruth

Ichiro Suzuki

Tiger Woods

SPORTS HEROES AND LEGENDS

Derek Jeter

by Keith Elliot Greenberg

BARNES & NOBLE BOOKS

NEW YORK

To Jennifer, Dylan, and Summer

Cover photograph:
© Rob Tringali/SportsChrome

Copyright © 2005 by Lerner Publications Company

This first edition published by Barnes & Noble Publishing, Inc., by arrangement with Lerner Publications Company, a division of Lerner Publishing Group, Minneapolis, MN.

Barnes & Noble Publishing, Inc.
122 Fifth Avenue
New York, NY 10011

ISBN 0–7607–6901–X

Printed and bound in the United States of America

05 06 07 08 09 BP 10 9 8 7 6 5 4 3 2 1

Sports Heroes and Legends™ is a trademark of Barnes & Noble Publishing, Inc.

Contents

Prologue

One in a Million

When Derek Jeter took the field on April 2, 1996, the New York Yankees had their full attention focused on him. Only a few years before, Jeter had been the top high school player in the country. After he spent four years in the Yankees' minor league system, the team's manager, Joe Torre, had decided that Jeter was ready for the big time. It was up to Jeter to prove Torre right.

The twenty-one-year-old shortstop appeared calm in the season opener, an away game against the Cleveland Indians. In the second inning, Jeter snared a grounder for an out, making the play look easy. Three innings later, he belted a home run off pitcher Dennis Martinez, putting the Yankees ahead 2–0.

Jeter had collected only sixteen homers in the minor leagues, so the big hit came as a surprise. "I wasn't looking for a home run, but it was a great feeling," he commented afterward.

The hit made him the first Yankee rookie to slam an opening day home run since Jerry Kennedy in 1969.

And Jeter wasn't done yet. In the fifth inning, Cleveland shortstop Omar Vizquel hit a ball that blooped toward left-center field. Jeter turned and took off with his back to home plate. The ball floated in the wind and Jeter moved with it, lunging to grab the ball over his left shoulder. The spectacular one-handed catch ended the inning for the Indians and kept the Yankees in command of the game. The Indians, who were the defending American League champions, lost to the Yankees 7–1.

New York fans took notice of Jeter's performance against the top team in the league, wondering if he might be able to lead the Yankees back to a league championship. Reporters were fascinated by the charming young shortstop, and Joe Torre didn't seem to mind at all. "I never get tired of talking about Derek Jeter," the manager said, "because he's a special kid who's all class."

The Yankees were about to find out just how special Jeter could be. But for those who knew him, the answer was obvious. His childhood friend Don Zomer Jr. summed it up, declaring, "He's one in a million."

Chapter One

The Youngest Yankee Fan

Derek Sanderson Jeter was born on June 26, 1974, in Pequannock, New Jersey—less than an hour's drive from New York's Yankee Stadium. Derek's Irish American mother, Dorothy, was an accountant. His African American father, Charles, was a social worker who specialized in treating patients with drug and alcohol problems.

ON THIS DAY IN HISTORY

On June 26, 1819—exactly 155 years before Derek Jeter's birth—Abner Doubleday was born. He was a Civil War hero, and he was declared the inventor of modern baseball. But recent historians doubt he created the game. Alexander Cartwright has since been credited with devising baseball as we know it.

Charles and Dorothy had met in 1972, while they were working for the U.S. Army in Frankfurt, Germany. Their families worried that the two might face challenges as an interracial couple, but Charles and Dorothy knew they could handle anything that came their way. They agreed that they would raise their children to appreciate their white heritage and their black heritage, encouraging them to make friends of all races.

When Derek was four years old, the family moved to Kalamazoo, Michigan. The following year, Derek's younger sister, Sharlee, was born. Although the siblings were five years apart, they became very close. Both children showed an early love for sports—especially baseball.

Each summer Derek and Sharlee would travel to New Jersey to visit their grandparents, Sonny and Dot Connors. Dot was one of the biggest baseball fans Derek knew. She loved the New York Yankees, and she took him to his first baseball game—a Yankees game, of course—when Derek was six years old. Neither Dot nor Derek can remember much about the game, but Dot is certain that the Yankees won.

Derek loved playing catch, and he knew he could always count on his grandmother to play with him. He would wake her early in the morning, saying, "C'mon, Gram, let's throw!" While Sharlee and Derek's visiting cousins slept, Derek and Dot would be out in the yard, practicing. Even when he was young, Derek had such a strong arm that his throw could almost knock over his grandmother.

Dot enjoyed telling Derek about the time she'd visited Yankee Stadium in 1948, days after Babe Ruth died. She'd walked past the Yankee hero's casket at home plate with thousands of other fans. In the 1930s and 1940s, she'd followed Yankees games on the radio, and she loved hearing the sound of Joe DiMaggio's bat smashing another hit.

BABE RUTH

Many people believe that George Herman Ruth Jr.—known as Babe Ruth—was the greatest baseball player who ever lived. He signed with the Boston Red Sox in 1914, when he was just nineteen years old. He played with the team as an outfielder and a pitcher until 1920, when he was traded to the New York Yankees. He led the Yankees to four World Series wins, and in 1927 he hit sixty home runs in a single season.

Derek told his grandmother and everyone else in his family that he was going to play for the Yankees one day. He treasured his Yankee windbreaker and the baseball that Yankee slugger Dave Winfield had autographed for him in the parking lot of Tiger Stadium in Detroit.

Not only was Winfield awesome on the field, he also went out of his way to make a difference outside of baseball. He started an organization called the Winfield Foundation to assist needy children. "I thought it was cool a major leaguer did a lot for kids," Derek said. "So I decided that if and when I made the majors, I wanted to do the same thing."

Derek's parents supported his love of baseball, and they encouraged him to work hard at everything he did. School was a huge priority in the family. Before the beginning of each school year, the Jeters sat down with their children to set goals for the year. The goals included grades, as well as what each child hoped to accomplish in sports. If anyone tried convincing the kids to take drugs, Derek and Sharlee were expected to say no. Each goal was written down on a yellow notepad. Then each child would sign the "contract."

Derek, who was known to his friends as "D.J.," made extra money by mowing neighbors' lawns. But since the ground in Michigan is covered by snow much of the year, this was a pretty limited job. Even though Derek tried winter sports like downhill skiing, he was frustrated that the long winters kept him from playing more baseball. He preferred to stay out of the cold, so he joined his school's basketball team to stay active.

Derek enjoyed watching sports of all kinds, and he followed the University of Michigan football team. But in most sports, he remained loyal to his East Coast roots. In basketball he cheered on the New York Knicks. And although most of the kids in Kalamazoo followed the Detroit Tigers, the Jeters went to Tiger Stadium to cheer for the Yankees whenever they were in town.

DAVE WINFIELD

Derek's childhood idol, Dave Winfield, is one of the most gifted athletes ever to play the game of baseball. After attending the University of Minnesota, he was drafted by four teams in three professional sports: the San Diego Padres (Major League Baseball), Minnesota Vikings (National Football League), Atlanta Hawks (National Basketball Association), and Utah Stars (the old American Basketball Association). The future Hall of Famer picked baseball and played for the Padres, Yankees, California Angels, Toronto Blue Jays, Minnesota Twins, and Cleveland Indians.

Derek's parents sent him to St. Augustine Cathedral School, where he got along with most of the other students. Once, when Derek teased a classmate, his parents scolded him and asked him to think about what he'd said. How would he feel if someone made the same remarks to him? Derek learned his lesson and didn't make the same mistake again. "I was just struck with how much he cared about his fellow classmates," said Shirley Garzelloni, Derek's fourth-grade teacher.

---

66 *As far back as I could remember, I always told my parents I wanted to be a baseball player. But they always told me education comes first.* 99

—DEREK JETER

Garzelloni recalled that Derek was somewhat shy but confident. He was a hard worker, and he consistently earned good grades. One year Derek wrote an essay describing his dream of playing shortstop for the New York Yankees. After school he could often be found playing baseball.

Derek loved to pitch, but Charles worried that the rigorous demands of the position might strain his son's arm. In addition, Charles knew he could teach Derek a lot more about other positions on the field—especially shortstop. Charles had played shortstop at Fisk University in Nashville, Tennessee. Because Derek idolized his father, shortstop quickly became his favorite position.

Many of the other kids in Kalamazoo didn't believe that Derek would ever realize his dream of becoming a major leaguer. "When I was growing up, everyone said that you can't do it, and they laughed at me," he said. But their doubts only made him more determined to prove them wrong.

A fence separated the Jeter backyard from the Kalamazoo Central High School baseball diamond. The entire family would often climb over the barrier to play ball together. Charles would pitch to Derek while Dorothy and Sharlee fielded. Then they'd switch to softball, and Sharlee would have her turn at bat. Sometimes Derek's father would give him fielding drills to help him become a better shortstop.

When Charles coached his son's Little League team one year, Derek found himself moved to second base. Derek's friend Josh Ewbank became the team's shortstop instead. Derek was confused, but Charles explained that he wanted his son to grow accustomed to playing a number of positions. "It seemed a lot of parents would encourage one part of the kid's game," Charles said. "I wanted him to be an all-around player. . . . I would tell him, 'You have to have more range if you want to play shortstop.'"

When his team was batting, Derek couldn't wait for his turn at the plate—particularly in tense situations. He looked forward to the chance to make the game-winning hit. Regardless of whether Derek was at the plate or in the field, he managed to command the attention of both adults and children. His love and enthusiasm for the game was infectious.

When no Little League games were scheduled, Derek and his friends played on their own in a small park near his home. They had a fire hydrant for first base, a pothole for second base, and a tree stump for third base. Because of Derek's advanced ability, he often found himself playing with older kids. It didn't matter. As long as everyone was focused on the game, Jeter was happy.

Star Potential

D erek was eager to make the most of his time in high school—athletically and academically. Before his freshman year, he tried out for the Kazoo Blues. The team was an elite basketball squad sponsored by the Amateur Athletic Union. Although baseball was Derek's first love, he was also a decent basketball player. Players from all over western Michigan were vying for a spot on the team. During tryouts it became clear that Derek didn't have the best basketball skills of the group, but the coach admired his willingness to hustle and work hard. Derek made the team.

In the spring when baseball tryouts rolled around, Derek was ready. Since he was only in his first year of high school, he tried out for the junior varsity team. He might have joined varsity right away, but Kalamazoo already had Craig Humphrey— an All-Conference shortstop and one of the team's best hitters.

Even so, Derek's play was so strong that he was promoted to varsity partway through the season. The coaches shifted Humphrey to second base to make room for their new shortstop.

After Derek's sophomore year of high school, he joined a summer traveling baseball team called the Kalamazoo Maroons. At age fifteen, he was the second-youngest player to make the team in its sixty-year history. Once again an older player had to be switched to second base to make room for Derek at shortstop. Derek was determined not to let the team down. Coach Dan Hinga recalls that Derek would show up early on game days and stay late after games, fielding grounders as long as someone would hit to him.

❝ *Baseball's a very humbling sport. You can go from top to bottom in one day.* ❞

—DEREK JETER

Despite Derek's strong showing on the field, he remained modest. Explained Jeter, "I don't like people who brag and talk about themselves all the time. I never really liked it, so I've never done it. I've known lots of people like that. It turns me off."

In fact, when Derek was in class, he barely mentioned baseball at all. During the school day, he focused completely on his studies. It was what his parents expected of him. Despite his busy schedule, Derek found time to join the National Honor Society and serve as president of the school's Latin Club.

Derek was so serious about school that his friends thought he would grow up to be a doctor. But the teenager couldn't get the Yankees out of his mind. A British literature teacher asked students to create a coat of arms unique to their personalities. In one corner of his design, Derek drew himself wearing a Yankees uniform.

Kalamazoo Central High School's colors are maroon and white, and the sports teams are known as the Maroon Giants.

One of Derek's classmates, Don Zomer Jr., was the son of the high school baseball coach. Don favored the New York Mets—the Yankees' crosstown rival in New York City. From time to time, the friends would argue about their team preferences. "Derek was always sure that he was going to play for the Yankees," Don recalled. "He said, 'You like the Mets, but when I'm playing shortstop for the Yankees, you'll change.'"

Anyone watching Derek on the field could see that he had real potential to end up in the major leagues. During his junior year, Derek had a .557 batting average and seven home runs. He opened his senior-year season by slamming three home runs in his first seven at bats. But a bad ankle sprain slowed him down, and he missed three games. While he hit only one more homer that season, his overall play was still spectacular. Coach Zomer was forced to switch around the infield to accommodate the young man's skills. "He would throw ninety-one, ninety-two miles an hour from short to first," Zomer said. "I had to put a better athlete at first just to handle his throws."

Zomer acknowledged that Derek had a lot of natural ability, but he believes Derek's work ethic really sets him apart from other ballplayers. "Derek was always asking me to hit him more ground balls," he recalled. "He was always the first one on the field, and the last one off."

Even though Derek was very busy studying and playing baseball during his high school years, he also found time to socialize. His mother remembers that he received a lot of phone calls—especially from girls!

By the end of Jeter's senior year, he'd broken many of the baseball records at Kalamazoo Central. He had a .508 batting average, and in twenty-three games he had 30 hits, 4 home runs, and 23 runs batted in (RBIs). He also stole twelve bases in twelve attempts. The American Baseball Coaches Association named him the 1992 High School Player of the Year. *USA Today* also selected him as its high school player of the year, and the state of Michigan named him "Mr. Baseball."

Derek's hot play was attracting notice across the nation. As many as two dozen baseball scouts would regularly fill the stands at Kalamazoo's games. University baseball programs and major league teams both expressed interest. While some baseball players sign with a major league team directly after high school, other players attend several years of college, refining their skills before taking a shot at the big leagues. Derek would have to decide which path was right for him.

Ace Adams, assistant baseball coach at the University of Michigan, met with the Jeter family in an effort to sign Derek up. Dorothy asked Adams whether he thought Derek was good enough to play for the team. "Mrs. Jeter," Adams answered, "he could've started here when he was in the eighth grade."

The Jeters liked everything they saw. "It was a good academic school," Derek said of the University of Michigan, "and school always came first."

Derek had no trouble getting accepted at the University of Michigan on a baseball scholarship. But the Major League Baseball 1992 amateur draft—an event for teams to pick new players—was scheduled for June 1, 1992. In the weeks beforehand, the Jeters realized that Derek was very popular with major league baseball scouts. In fact, twenty-seven out of baseball's twenty-eight teams contacted them about the possibility of drafting Derek.

Unfortunately, the one team that didn't appear interested was the Yankees. But two days before the draft, the phone rang in the Jeter home. It was Yankee scout Dick Groch. He'd been watching Derek closely for two years, he said. But he hadn't wanted to disrupt the family's life by contacting him while he was still busy with high school.

---

66 *He's going to Cooperstown.* 99
—DICK GROCH, PREDICTING THAT DEREK JETER WILL ONE DAY
BE INDUCTED INTO BASEBALL'S HALL OF FAME

The Yankees had the sixth pick in the first round of the draft. That meant five other teams had a chance to select Derek before the Yankees. But choosing a high school player can be risky for a team. A high schooler nearly always needs a few years in the minor leagues before he's ready for the majors. And a struggling team may not want to wait that long to bring in fresh talent. For that reason, college players can be more attractive. In addition, a player's position can affect when he's drafted. A team with a decent shortstop and a weak pitching staff would be much more likely to draft a pitcher as its first round pick. As it turned out, the first five teams all picked college players. When the Yankees' turn came, they made the first high school pick of the draft—Derek Jeter!

As soon as Derek and the Yankees worked out the contract negotiations, Derek would be on his way to the minor leagues. While Derek was thrilled about being drafted by the Yankees, getting a college education was still important to him. Derek's contract with the Yankees included a clause that guaranteed the team would pay for Derek to attend college once he was ready.

❞ *It was an honor to be picked high and to be picked by New York. . . . Playing in the pros has always been my dream.* ❟

—DEREK JETER

A month after the draft, Derek signed a contract giving him a $700,000 signing bonus and caught a flight to Florida to join the Yankees' Rookie League team. He was about to find out if he could make it as a professional ballplayer.

Chapter Three

Paying His Dues

Even though Jeter was younger and less experienced than most of his new teammates, he felt ready for the minor leagues. "I pretty much have been playing with older players all my life," he said, "so I'm used to it."

Jeter had his first chance to show off his skills on his second day in Florida, July 2, 1992. He played both games of a doubleheader with his new team, the Gulf Coast League Yankees. He went 0 for 7 at the plate with five strikeouts. It was a big change from high school, when he'd struck out only once during his senior year. The pitchers were much tougher, and the whole game moved at a faster pace. "The pitches looked like Tic Tacs," he recalled.

Jeter spent much of his spare time at the team's hotel in Tampa, trying to rest. His father had advised him to sleep as much as possible and save his energy for games. He missed his parents badly and, in some ways, considered their two visits to Tampa the high points of his season. The minor leagues "are not as easy as people may think," he said. "You get used to playing every day, being on the road, living out of a suitcase. It's a tough experience."

During his first year in the minor leagues, Derek was so homesick that he called his parents in Michigan several times a day. His phone bills averaged almost $400 a month!

In Jeter's six weeks in the Rookie League, his batting average was .202. He struggled on defense as well, making multiple errors in nearly every game he played. But the coaches remained supportive. They'd seen many players struggle to adjust to the minor leagues, and they were confident Jeter would improve over time. When the Gulf Coast League season came to an end, the Yankees sent Jeter to their Class A team in Greensboro, North Carolina. During his two weeks with the Greensboro Hornets, his batting average was .243. Things were looking up. But Jeter knew the path to the major leagues wouldn't be easy. "I need to work on everything," he told a reporter, "defense, offense, baserunning. I don't feel like I've mastered anything yet."

Jeter took a break from baseball in the fall, and he returned to Ann Arbor for a semester at the University of Michigan. He enjoyed being around other people his age, cheering for the Wolverines at football and basketball games and feeling like a normal student. The time away from the pressures of the minor leagues helped Jeter refocus and prepare to return to the game he loved.

The Minor Leagues

Major league baseball teams each have a system of minor league teams, and most players must work their way up the system, gaining experience before appearing in the big leagues. Typically, a player first reports to rookie league, followed by Class A, Class AA, and Class AAA. A player may spend anywhere from a few weeks to a few years at a given level.

Jeter began the 1993 season back at Class A Greensboro. At first it appeared that he was going to have another tough year in the field. His footwork was inconsistent, and he couldn't seem to get his arm under control. He frequently overshot his throw to first base, which prevented the first baseman from making the out and gave the runner a chance to get to second base. In the first half of the season, Jeter racked up thirty-five errors. "I was making errors every day," he recalled. "I was saying, 'Maybe they won't hit another ground ball to shortstop.'"

But the first part of the season had a few highlights as well. In April the Hornets were playing the Augusta Pirates. The game was tied 9–9 in the ninth inning when Jeter stepped up to bat. With the count at 0–2 (no balls and two strikes), he slammed a game-winning home run. In June Jeter's batting average was up to .337, and he and four of his teammates were selected to take part in the South Atlantic League All-Star game.

❝For me, 0–2 is my favorite count. It makes me concentrate more because I don't like to strike out.❞

—DEREK JETER

At about that time, the Yankees sent Gene Michael, a veteran shortstop, to give Jeter some one-on-one coaching. Michael analyzed Jeter's play and advised him to study Baltimore Orioles shortstop Cal Ripkin Jr. Whenever Ripkin made a smooth play, Derek imagined himself in the same position. Michael pointed out that Ripkin used a consistent technique to get to the ball and make the throw every time the ball came his way. Jeter, on the other hand, was using a different technique for every play.

GENE MICHAEL

Gene Michael spent seven years with the Yankees. He was the team's main shortstop for five of those years, starting in 1968. He also pitched one game, hurling three shutout innings. His lanky 6'2" frame earned him the nickname "Stick."

Jeter ended the season with a solid .295 batting average. That average was the fifth highest in the Yankee organization. But baseball teams typically rely on shortstops for their great defensive skills—not their offensive skills. Fortunately, Jeter's fielding had been steadily improving. In the second half of the season, his errors were down to twenty-one. More important, he'd attracted the attention of *Baseball America,* a magazine that covers the minor leagues. It voted him the league's best infield arm, best defensive shortstop, and most exciting player.

Despite Jeter's improvements, rumors were circulating that the Yankees might move him to third base or the outfield. At the end of the regular season, the Yankees sent Jeter to the Fall Instructional League to focus on his fielding. Instructional League classes meet seven days a week for five weeks. That's thirty-five days of nonstop baseball!

Derek was determined not to lose his favorite position on the field. Coach Brian Butterfield helped Jeter eliminate his bad habits. Jeter took a more aggressive stance when a ball came his way, stepping toward the ball instead of backing up. He stopped jerking his glove around and developed a more efficient throw to first base.

 In Derek's twenty games in the Fall Instructional League, he made only one error.

The extra training helped him transform into one of the standout players of the 1994 minor leagues. Jeter began the year playing for Class A Tampa in the Florida State League. By mid-May he had a .308 batting average and led the team with twelve stolen bases. After reaching a .329 average in sixty-nine games, the Yankees promoted Jeter to the Class AA team in Albany, New York. There he hit .377 in thirty-four games and was named Eastern League Player of the Month in July. As a result, he finished the season with the Class AAA club in Ohio, the Columbus Clippers. Derek's mother, Dorothy, was even able to drive from Kalamazoo to watch his first game with the Clippers. Dorothy could see that Derek had finally hit his stride.

In three different leagues, Jeter averaged .344 and had 5 home runs, 68 RBIs, and a whopping 50 stolen bases! Best of all, he was down to 25 errors for the season. *Baseball America, The Sporting News, USA Today, Baseball Weekly,* and Topps/NAPBL (National Association of Professional Baseball Leagues) all chose Derek as Minor League Player of the Year. He looked ready for the major leagues.

But there was one problem—the major league players were on strike. Players and owners couldn't reach agreements on several financial matters. The 1994 season ended in August, and the World Series was canceled. Jeter headed off for the Arizona Fall League, where he injured his shoulder. He spent the winter recovering and wondering about his future.

PLAYING WITH MIKE

One of the highlights of Jeter's Arizona Fall League play was facing Michael Jordan. The Chicago Bulls superstar had put his basketball career on hold, and in 1994 he played with the Class AA Birmingham Barons. He had a .202 average with 3 home runs and 51 RBIs.

Major league players and owners resolved their differences in the off-season, and when March 1995 rolled around, the big leagues were back in business. Derek began the season with the Columbus Clippers. In May 1995, he finally made it to "The Show," as the major leagues are called. Tony Fernandez, the Yankees' starting shortstop, had strained a rib cage muscle. The club's second baseman, Pat Kelly, had a sprained wrist, and the team needed an extra player to put on the field. While Fernandez and Kelly recuperated, Derek would be a New York Yankee.

On May 29, Derek traveled to Seattle, Washington, where the Yankees faced the Mariners. Charles Jeter woke up at 3 AM so he could fly out to be in the stands for his son's major league debut. Dorothy stayed in Kalamazoo to attend Sharlee's high school softball game. The Jeters wanted their children to know that both of their games were equally important.

THE SEATTLE MARINERS

The Seattle Mariners were founded in 1977. The team struggled in its early years, but the Mariners began to win more games in 1993 when Lou Piniella took over as manager. The team played its home games in a stadium called the Kingdome. Top Mariners players in 1995 included pitcher Randy Johnson, designated hitter Edgar Martinez, and outfielders Jay Buhner and Ken Griffey Jr.

In Derek's first appearance as a Yankee, he played well in the field but struggled at the plate. The Yankees blew two leads, and at the end of the ninth inning, the game was tied 7–7. In the eleventh inning, with two outs and the go-ahead (tie-breaking) run on third base, Derek stepped up to bat. He struck out. He was 0–5 in the major leagues, and the Yankees lost the game.

Afterward Charles and Derek went out for dinner and talked about the game. Derek focused on what he wanted to do in his game the next day. In that game, Derek notched his first two major league hits (both singles) and scored two of the team's three runs. It wasn't enough to turn the game around, though, and the Yanks lost 7–3.

> **❝** *I was worried about how I played, and worried about going home. . . . Now, I realize that when you play 140 games, there will always be another game tomorrow. So now, I try to make it fun. A lot of people take it too much as a job. But it's a game, and you still have to have fun.* **❞**
>
> —DEREK JETER

In early June, Fernandez rejoined the team at second base, allowing Jeter to stay in the big leagues. But after a few games, the Yankees moved Fernandez back to shortstop, and Jeter had to return to Columbus. In thirteen major league games, Derek hit .234 and had six RBIs.

In September, after the Clippers finished their season, the Yankees called up Derek again. Manager Buck Showalter wanted to give Jeter the chance to observe more big league games so he'd be ready when his chance came to play regularly. Jeter appeared in only two games but managed to raise his major league batting average to .250.

In the meantime, he'd had a strong season with the Clippers, batting .317—the highest of any Yankee minor league player in 1995—and slamming 154 hits. He'd obviously outgrown the minor leagues, and team officials knew it. The only question that remained was how soon Jeter would be wearing a Yankees uniform full-time.

Chapter Four

Taking Nothing for Granted

The Yankees started off 1996 with a new manager, Joe Torre. At spring training, Torre had to choose between Jeter and Fernandez at shortstop. Shortstop was one of the least secure positions on the Yankee team—in the previous five years, five different men had started the season at short. In late March, Fernandez broke his elbow while making a tough catch. As a result, Derek became the first rookie to begin the season at shortstop for the New York Yankees since Tom Tresh in 1962.

Interestingly, Jeter was issued number two—one of only two single-digit numbers not retired by the team. (The other number—six—belonged to Torre.) The other players who'd worn single-digit numbers are all featured in Monument Park, an area behind the outfield dedicated to past Yankees legends.

In the team's ninety-three-year history, the Yankees had won twenty-two World Series championships—more than any other team in baseball. But the team had struggled in recent years. In 1995 the Bronx Bombers made it to the playoffs for the first time in fourteen years, only to get knocked out by the Seattle Mariners in the first round. Owner George Steinbrenner was hoping that a new manager and young, exciting players like Derek Jeter could give the team the edge it needed to make it back to the top.

JOE TORRE

When Joe Torre took over as Yankees manager, he already knew a lot about baseball in New York City. After growing up in Brooklyn, he spent eighteen years in the major leagues playing for the Braves (in Milwaukee and Atlanta), the St. Louis Cardinals, and the New York Mets. His experiences as an All-Star catcher and a first and third baseman helped him during the next fourteen years, when he had stints as manager for each of those same three teams.

Derek felt ready for the big time, but he was still a youngster on a team of superstars that included Cecil Fielder, Darryl Strawberry, David Cone, and Dwight Gooden. He needed to prove he belonged. Jeter reassured any doubters when he blasted his opening-day home run off Indians pitcher Dennis

Martinez. The following night, Jeter gave an equally stellar performance, getting three hits and scoring three runs to help his team to a 5–1 victory over Cleveland.

The Yankees built on their strong start, charging to the lead in their division. On May 14, pitcher Dwight Gooden was on his way to a no-hitter against the Mariners when he needed a little help from his teammates. In the bottom of the ninth inning with two outs, Mariner Paul Sorrento hit a fly to short-left field. Jeter ran back and made the catch for the final out of the game, making it the ninth no-hitter in Yankee history.

Throughout the 1996 season, Jeter continued to impress. On August 2 in Kansas City, the Yankees played a close game against the Royals that went into extra innings. In the tenth, Jeter hit a line drive over the head of center fielder Tom Goodwin. It bounced off the stadium's back wall and Jeter rounded the bases before Goodwin could throw the ball back to the infield. It was the first Yankee inside-the-park home run in six years.

Jeter played a total of 157 games during the season, including 106 in a row. During the second half, he hit an amazing .350. Another high point was a seventeen-game hitting streak. That year Jeter had no permanent spot in the team's lineup—on some days he hit leadoff and on others he hit ninth. Regardless of his position in the batting order, Jeter seemed to be a key ingredient in every Yankee rally.

HIGH HOPES

At the beginning of the 1996 season, Torre told reporters that he would be content if Derek hit .250. When Charles Jeter heard those words, he predicted that Torre would be pleasantly surprised at the end of the year. "I was saying to myself, 'I know Derek is not going to be satisfied with . . . .250.'"

Of course Derek also had a few awkward moments—on and off the field. Less than two weeks after his inside-the-park homer, Jeter and the Yankees were playing the Chicago White Sox. In the top of the eighth with two outs, slugger Cecil Fielder was at bat and Jeter was on second base. Jeter attempted to steal third and was thrown out, ending his team's rally. The White Sox went on to win.

One morning in Manhattan, Derek awoke to discover that his new car had been stolen. "I parked it on Second Avenue," he said. "Usually, I park it in the garage. I guess it was a rookie mistake."

But Jeter kept a positive attitude. Rather than worrying about mistakes he couldn't go back and change, he kept moving forward. After Jeter performed poorly in one game, Torre was asked if he had a talk with the rookie. "I didn't need to,"

Torre replied. "He's not a kid who needs that kind of direction. He's the kind of kid you never have to worry about."

When the regular season ended, Jeter had hit .314, with 10 home runs and 78 RBIs. He also led the Yankees with 183 hits. He was the first full-time shortstop to pull off a batting average above .300 since 1956, when Gil McDougald hit .311. He also had more RBIs than any Yankee shortstop since 1936, when Frank Crosetti also had 78.

Best of all, the Yankees were in first place and headed to the playoffs. The first round of the playoffs, the American League Division Series (ALDS), includes the top teams from the league's three divisions, East, Central, and West, and one wild-card team. (The wild-card spot goes to the team with the best overall record that is not first place in its division.) The ALDS determines which two teams will face each other in the second round, the American League Championship Series (ALCS). The winner of that series goes on to face the winner of the National League Championship Series (NLCS) in the World Series.

The Yankees took on the Texas Rangers in the ALDS, a best-of-five series. The Rangers won the first game, 6–2. In game two, the Yankees fought to take the lead, but after nine innings, the game was tied. In the twelfth inning, Jeter scored the winning run. That win gave the Yankees the confidence they needed to take the next two games and win the series, 3–1.

In the ALCS against the Baltimore Orioles, Derek found himself in the midst of a truly unusual controversy. In the eighth inning of game one, with the Orioles leading 4–3, Jeter came to bat against Baltimore pitcher Armando Benitez. Jeter launched a shot toward Yankee Stadium's right-field bleachers, and Orioles right fielder Tony Tarasco positioned himself at the wall, ready to make the catch. Suddenly Jeff Maier, a twelve-year-old Yankee fan from New Jersey, reached over the wall with his own glove, deflecting the ball into the bleachers. As Tarasco looked on in shock, right-field umpire Rich Garcia ruled that Jeter had hit a home run.

The game, now tied, continued into extra innings, and the Yankees eventually won the matchup in the eleventh on a home run by Bernie Williams. To Yankee supporters, the Maier incident symbolized the good fortune that the team had enjoyed over the years. To others, the episode represented the lucky breaks that the Yankees didn't deserve. For a few days, Maier was a hero in the New York area. But ultimately the attention shifted back to the ballplayers.

Baltimore won game two of the series, but New York took the next two. The ALCS is best-of-seven games, so the Yankees needed one more win to clinch it. The championship series ended with Derek fielding a slow-rolling ball off the bat of thirty-six-year-old Cal Ripkin Jr. As Ripkin slid headfirst into first base, the rookie managed to throw him out. Many saw this as a passing of the torch. Ripkin, the greatest shortstop of his time, saw his team's hopes die at the hands of the shortstop of tomorrow.

Jeter could hardly believe his luck. His team was just four wins away from a World Championship. Derek had been seven years old the last time that the Yankees had been in the World Series. He remembered because that was the year his favorite player, Dave Winfield, had joined the team. But even with the great Winfield, the Yankees lost that year. During practice on the day before game one of the 1996 World Series, Jeter ducked into the dugout to grab a bat. Suddenly he saw Winfield. The two shook hands, and Jeter was in for another surprise. Winfield had become a Derek Jeter fan!

The Yankees faced the defending world champions, the Atlanta Braves, in the series. Many predicted the Braves would win, especially after they crushed the Yankees 12–1 in game one. Game two wasn't much better, with the Yankees suffering a 4–0 loss. To make matters worse, Greg Maddox nailed Jeter's left wrist with a pitch. Whenever his teammates were batting, Jeter wrapped his wrist in ice to relieve the pain, but he refused to sit out the rest of the game, afraid of missing even a moment of the action.

❝ *This is the best time I ever had in my life. I can't imagine wanting anything else.* ❞

—DEREK JETER

The Yankees finally turned things around in game three, with a 5–2 win. Atlanta charged ahead in game four, leading 6–0 after five innings. But the Yankees came alive in the sixth, scoring three runs. They followed up with another three runs in the eighth to tie the game. The Yankees finished off the Braves in the tenth and won 8–6. The Braves had blown their two-game lead, and two losses in a row had shaken their confidence.

The Yankees pitching staff put together their best perform-ance in game five, and the Yanks won 1–0. To end the series, players returned to Yankee Stadium, where the New York fans were determined to cheer their team to victory. In game six, the Yankees scored three runs in the third inning and, despite their best efforts, the Braves never caught up. In the fourth inning, with the bases loaded, Braves designated hitter Terry Pendleton hit an easy grounder straight to Derek Jeter, who turned it into a double play. The Yankees began the ninth inning with a one-run lead, and that inning ended when Yankees third baseman Charlie Hayes caught a foul pop-up with the bases loaded. With a final score of 3–2, the Yankees had won their first World Series in eighteen years!

Although Jeter had played fifteen games with the Yankees in 1995, he was still considered a rookie for the 1996 season.

Jeter was truly a marvel. While many solid players choke under the postseason pressure, Jeter only improved. His post-season batting average was .361. He had racked up three RBIs and scored twelve runs. If that wasn't enough, the Baseball

Writers' Association of America unanimously voted Jeter American League Rookie of the Year. He was the first Yankee to earn the prize since pitcher Dave Righetti in 1981. He won not only because of his personal accomplishments but because he was a key player in the Yankees' rise to the top.

It almost seemed too much for a twenty-two-year-old kid from Kalamazoo. But he wasn't complaining. "If it's too much too soon," he told an interviewer, "I hope I get too much every year."

Chapter Five

Turn 2

Jeter began the off-season by joining the rest of the Yankees in a victory parade through Manhattan. Jeter enjoyed the celebration, but soon he began thinking seriously about the future. He announced to his father that he wanted to start a foundation. With help from Charles, Derek started the Turn 2 Foundation, dedicated to promoting healthy lifestyles among young people.

The expression "Turn 2" is baseball slang for double play. But for Jeter it also has another meaning. He wants kids to "turn to" his foundation and "turn away" from substance abuse. The foundation began by holding events in Michigan and in New York. "It wasn't too long ago that I was a kid," Jeter explained. "I looked up to professional athletes, so I think if you're in that position, you should try to do something positive with it. Kids are the leaders of the future."

Jeter made sure that the foundation had a strong leadership program. It rewarded youngsters for academic accomplishments, as well as for being active in their communities. The kids who became involved with Turn 2 attended leadership conferences and were encouraged to speak to their peers about leading a healthy and positive lifestyle.

Naturally, the foundation held baseball clinics. And it launched a Turn 2 after-school program, emphasizing physical fitness along with art, drama, dance, and other types of education. The group arranged for police and probation officers to speak about the consequences of drug use and organized trips to places where kids could see people working in interesting careers. Jeter hoped that his foundation would help kids to stay away from drugs and alcohol and realize all of the positive possibilities that existed for them.

In January 1997, Jeter and teammate Bernie Williams had small roles on the hit TV show *Seinfeld*. Derek boasted, "I had two lines and Bernie only got one."

When he wasn't busy setting up his foundation, Jeter found himself slipping the video of the final game of the World Series into his VCR. "Every time I see Charlie Hayes catch that last ball,

I get chills," he said. "We were like a family the whole year. When I watch that videotape, it's like we scaled the mountain together."

Some fans worried that Jeter might fall victim to the "sophomore slump" and have trouble maintaining his high level of play during his second full year in the major leagues. "Everyone's talking about it," Jeter admitted. "It makes me work that much harder." That hard work was a key part of Jeter's plan to avoid any dip in his performance on the field. He spent eight weeks going through an intensive training program to add power to his swing. By the time he showed up at spring training, Jeter had gained fifteen pounds of muscle.

JETER THE MAILMAN

During spring training, Jeter was frequently spotted answering fan mail. "My rookie year, I'd put it off for a week, and I couldn't find my glove behind all the envelopes," he observed. "Now, I make a conscious effort to do it every day."

From the moment Jeter arrived at the Yankees training center, it seemed that everyone was watching him. His salary had tripled since the year before, and Yankees owner George Steinbrenner wanted to make sure Jeter earned every penny. New

York newspapers had named him the most eligible bachelor in the city, so his actions off the field were monitored just as closely as his actions on it. But Jeter said the pressure didn't bother him.

His relaxed attitude resulted in a productive second year in the major leagues. After opening the season with two hitless games, Jeter quickly racked up thirteen hits in his next eighteen at bats, bringing his average up to .500. Jeter started in 159 out of 162 regular season games for the team, hitting .291 with ten home runs and seventy RBIs. In fifty-seven games, Jeter had multiple hits, leading the team in that category. He was also the first Yankee since Joe DiMaggio to score more than one hundred runs in his first two seasons.

The Yankees had a fairly strong year, but they finished second in the AL East behind the Baltimore Orioles. Even so, they managed to snag the wild-card spot, and Jeter found himself back in the playoffs. They faced the Cleveland Indians in the division series. In the sixth inning of game one, Yankee Tim Raines hit a home run. Jeter came up next, and he hit another homer. Then Paul O'Neill followed with the third Yankee home run in a row. It was the first time a team had ever hit back-to-back-to-back home runs in the major league playoffs!

Even though the Yankees began the ALDS with a win, they lost games two, three, and five, allowing Cleveland to advance. Jeter played well, starting all five playoff games and hitting .333, but he was disappointed in his team's overall performance. Next year, he told himself, he'd be back in the World Series.

 In 1997 Jeter helped turn eighty-seven double plays!

To prepare for 1998, Jeter bought a home in Tampa near the Yankees' training facility. Only five years earlier, he'd played rookie ball in the city, constantly complaining to his parents about the heat. But he'd grown to enjoy the warm winters, and Tampa was the best place to improve his game during the off-season.

In addition to lifting weights that winter, Jeter spent a lot of time with Gary Denbo, the Yankees' minor league hitting coordinator. Noting that Jeter had fared poorly against the Seattle Mariners in 1997, Jeter and Denbo discussed ways to remedy the problem. They concluded that the team's pitchers had confused Jeter with inside fastballs. Jeter changed to a more upright posture and tweaked his swing. This allowed him to pull more inside pitches to left field, rather than aiming them at right field. "I wanted to be able to turn on those pitches," Jeter said, "to be quicker inside, to drive those balls and not give up on them."

At spring training in 1998, Jeter's training paid off. He hit .394, with five homers and twenty RBIs. Jeter attracted more attention that year than ever before, especially when he revealed he was dating pop superstar Mariah Carey. Reporters and gossip columnists wrote article after article about the couple. But Jeter quickly tired of the media frenzy—he wanted to focus on baseball and keep his personal life out of the spotlight. Still, the attention proved he'd reached a whole new level of stardom.

Jeter has said that in New York, a city known for its racial diversity, he has an advantage coming from a multiracial background. "I can relate to everyone," he noted.

Pitcher David Cone compared traveling with Jeter to touring with the rock band the Beatles, who drew huge, adoring crowds wherever they went. "You'd think he was Ringo with all these girls screaming," Cone said, referring to the band's drummer Ringo Starr. Jeter had become the most popular Yankee in the eyes of many New Yorkers. In addition to his $750,000 salary, he earned hundreds of thousands of dollars endorsing products like soda pop, athletic gear, and a credit card.

The 1998 regular season got off to a slow start with five losses in a row. In the first ten games, Jeter could muster only a .200 average. Then everything seemed to fall into place, and the

Yankees shot back up in the standings. By mid-May they had a record of twenty-eight wins and nine losses—the second-best start ever by the team. As the weather warmed up, so did Jeter's bat. For the month of May, he hit .336 with four home runs and five doubles. His strong performance earned him Player of the Month honors from *Sports Illustrated*. By this time his relationship with Mariah Carey was over, but his name didn't seem likely to disappear from the headlines anytime soon.

The whole team got an extra dose of excitement on May 17, in a game against the Minnesota Twins. Pitcher David Wells accomplished one of the rarest feats in baseball—a perfect game. Wells had no hits, no walks, no batters who got to base on errors, and no hit batters. Every pop fly was caught. Every grounder was fielded and tossed to first base in time to throw the runner out. It was only the thirteenth perfect game in the twentieth century and only the second for the Yankees.

One reason for the team's success was newcomer Chuck Knoblauch. Knoblauch was a top-notch second baseman who had spent seven years with the Minnesota Twins. He'd won the Gold Glove—the award for the league's best fielder at his position—in 1997. He and Derek quickly developed a strong chemistry—especially for turning the double play. Knoblauch was also an excellent hitter and base stealer. With Knoblauch leading off and Derek batting second, the Yankees had a dangerous combination of speed and power at the top of their lineup.

Jeter spent two weeks in June on the disabled list with a strained abdominal muscle. Jeter came back from his injury raring to go, and in July he got his first taste of the All-Star game. Fan votes determine which players will start the game, which pits the AL against the NL. The All-Star team managers select backup players to round out the teams. Jeter finished second in the voting for AL shortstop, behind Mariners hotshot Alex Rodriguez, and he was selected as a backup. But Jeter didn't get much playing time.

RODRIGUEZ AND JETER

Alex Rodriguez, nicknamed A-Rod, and Derek Jeter faced comparisons with each other from the moment they both became full-time major league shortstops in 1996. The two had become friends years earlier, in 1992, when Alex—a high school senior in Florida—sought advice from Derek about life in the minor leagues. While the media debated which young man was the better shortstop, Jeter and Rodriguez simply ignored all the fuss. In A-Rod's first full year in the majors, he had a .358 batting average with 36 home runs and 123 RBIs. Derek, however, had a World Series ring.

In August, Jeter batted .382 and was named AL Player of the Month. He was the first Yankee to collect fifty hits in a single month since Joe DiMaggio had fifty-three in July 1941.

On September 9, the Yankees faced the Red Sox at Boston's Fenway Park. If the Yanks could pull off another win, they'd clinch the top spot in their division, guaranteeing a trip back to the playoffs. Jeter wasn't about to let his team down. In the first inning he smashed a home run against Boston's Tim Wakefield. When Jeter faced Wakefield again two innings later, the Yankee knocked out another homer. O'Neill helped the Yankee cause with two home runs of his own. When the game was over, the Yankees celebrated their 7–5 win by rushing past the disappointed Red Sox fans and into the clubhouse, where they doused one another with celebratory champagne.

At the end of the regular season, the Yankees had a league-leading record and an all-time club record of 114 wins. Jeter's stats were his best yet, with a .324 average, 19 homers, and 84 RBIs. He'd set a record for the most homers by a Yankee shortstop, and he was top in the league with 127 runs scored. He was especially proud that he'd made only nine errors in the entire season!

The Yankees hit a total of 207 home runs in 1998.

After eliminating the Texas Rangers with a three-game sweep of the ALDS, the Yankees faced the Cleveland Indians for the league title. Since the Indians had knocked them out in 1997, the Yanks were out for revenge. They got what they wanted, beating Cleveland four games to two. Jeter's best moment came in game six of the series, when he hit a two-run triple that helped the team to a 9–5 win.

" *Tell them, it wasn't easy. When they look back and see one-hundred-twenty-five wins, tell them we never took a single one for granted. Teach them about our passion and our patience. If they ask who was our star, give them twenty-five names. And if you forget our names, just tell them we were YANKEES. And in the season of our lives, we became a team. A team that made people believe that baseball could be magic, and men could be perfect.* **"**

—THE 1998 YANKEES

To win it all, the Yankees just had to get past the National League champs, the San Diego Padres. New York had an awesome series, sweeping the Padres in four straight games. Including the postseason, the Yankees had compiled a 125–50 record. Some fans and sportswriters began calling the 1998

Yankees the best team ever. As always, Jeter made great contributions to his team, and his World Series batting average was an impressive .353.

In his first three years in Major League Baseball, Derek had taken home two World Championships. Reporters wanted to know how he felt about that special achievement. "I've been spoiled," he replied.

Chapter Six

It Never Gets Old

Shortly before the 1998 playoffs, Derek began a streak, reaching base safely at least once during every remaining regular season game. When the 1999 season began, he picked up exactly where he left off. From September 24, 1998 to June 5, 1999, Jeter reached base safely in fifty-seven straight games.

But early in 1999, the Yankees struggled to focus on baseball after Joe Torre was diagnosed with prostate cancer. Torre underwent treatment and was back on the job within a few months. Hundreds of well-wishers send cards and flowers during his recovery.

 Derek came out with his very own breakfast cereal in 1999, called "Jeter's Frosted Flake Cereal."

On July 16, Jeter arrived at Yankee Stadium to find a crowd of reporters waiting for him. They wanted to check out a rumor that Jeter had been shot and rushed to a hospital. The news came as a complete surprise to Jeter. "I wasn't shot today, as far as I know," he joked. "I better call my mom, huh?"

WATCH OUT FOR THE ROCKET

When pitching ace Roger Clemens, nicknamed "the Rocket," joined the Yankees in 1999, Jeter was wary. While he played for the Red Sox, Clemens had a bad habit of hitting Jeter with fastballs. So when Jeter and his pal Chuck Knoblauch came out for their first batting practice with Clemens pitching, they wore full suits of catcher's gear!

Two days later, the Yankees held Yogi Berra Day to celebrate the star catcher, who was with the team from 1946 to 1963. Berra had the distinction of having caught Don Larsen's perfect game during the 1956 World Series. To commemorate the occasion, Larsen threw the ceremonial first pitch to Berra before the game began. Seeing those two Yankee heroes in action brought out the best in the 1999 team. David Cone amazed everyone that day by throwing a perfect game—the team's second perfect game in two years! In that game, Jeter also gave his best, blasting his sixteenth homer of the season over the left-center-field fence.

Soon afterward, the Yankees had their biggest win of the season. They crushed the Cleveland Indians 21–1. The Yanks hadn't scored that many runs in a home game since 1931, back when Babe Ruth and Lou Gehrig were both playing. That win gave the Yankees the best record in the major leagues, putting them ahead of the Indians by two games.

Throughout the year, Derek had six separate hitting streaks of ten games or more. He also reached career highs in batting (.349), home runs (24), RBIs (102), and walks (91). For the fourth straight year, he led the Yankees in hits (219). With each achievement, Derek gained a wider legion of fans. *People* magazine even named him one of its "50 Most Beautiful People in the World" that year.

The Yankees finished first in the AL East again in 1999. They had an easy time with the Texas Rangers in the ALDS, sweeping them in three games. In the battle for the ALCS, the Yankees found themselves squaring off against their historic adversaries, the Boston Red Sox.

The Red Sox took an early three-run lead in game one, but the Yanks fought back. Jeter tied up the game in the seventh inning with an RBI single. The Yankees finally secured the win with a Bernie Williams home run in the tenth inning. New York squeaked by again in game two, winning 3–2. The series then moved to Boston for the next two games. The Red Sox came alive on their home turf and pulled off a 13–1 win in game three. But the Yankees roared back in game four, pounding the Sox 9–2. Boston fans didn't let their team go quietly. When Sox shortstop Nomar Garciaparra was called out in a close play at first base in the ninth inning, spectators threw bottles and other litter onto the field. The Yankees retreated to their dugout until the fans settled down.

RED SOX RIVALRY

According to legend, the rivalry between the Boston Red Sox and the New York Yankees began in 1920. That year the Sox traded a young player named Babe Ruth, nicknamed "the Bambino," to the Yankees. The Red Sox didn't win another World Series for the rest of the twentieth century. With Ruth's help, the Yankees became one of the greatest teams of all time. The Red Sox blamed their string of losses on "the Curse of the Bambino." The rivalry has endured ever since.

The Yankees still had to play one more game in Boston before they were through. If they won, they'd be on their way to the World Series. Jeter came to bat in the first inning. On a 2–1 count, the shortstop cracked the ball 410 feet over Fenway Park's left-field fence. Jeter nearly had a second homer in the third inning, but his long ball flew just to the right of the right-field foul pole. The game ended with a score of 6–1, and the Yankees celebrated their third American League championship in four seasons. "Every year is special," Derek commented. "It never gets old."

 Fenway Park's famous left-field fence is known as the "Green Monster." It is 37 feet tall and 310 feet away from home plate.

The Yankees faced the Atlanta Braves in the World Series—a familiar opponent from 1996. The Braves had just beat the New York Mets to win the NLCS, and they were eager to take down the Big Apple's other baseball team. Game one was close until the eighth inning. Then Jeter stepped up to bat with the bases loaded and no outs. He hit a solid single and drove in one run. The Yanks went on to score three more runs that inning, giving them a 4–1 lead. The Braves never caught up.

New York made game two look even easier, scoring three runs in the first inning. Atlanta never challenged them, and they went on to win 7–2. Game three was close, but four homers by three different Yankees were enough to help their team to a 6–5 win. One more win would give the Yankees their second World Series sweep in a row. Jeter, who had continued hitting consistently, wanted to make sure he made his mark. In game four, Jeter rapped out a single, tying Hank Bauer's record of a seventeen-game postseason hitting streak. He then stole second base and scored a run off a Tino Martinez hit. A few innings later, Jeter made a great play in the field, foiling a Braves rally attempt. The Yankees ended the series as they began it, with a 4–1 win. The Yankees had won their twenty-fifth World Championship of the twentieth century!

***

66 *We just want to win. That's the bottom line. I think a lot of times people may become content with one championship or a little bit of success, but we don't really reflect on what we've done in the past. We focus on the present.* 99

—DEREK JETER

***

The twenty-five-year-old Jeter was the youngest Yankee to have accumulated three World Championships since Mickey Mantle (at age twenty-one) and Joe DiMaggio (at age twenty-three).

Jeter had a .353 average for the series and .375 total for the postseason.

As usual, Derek spent the winter conditioning himself for the upcoming season, this time adding eighteen pounds to his frame with weight training. He'd lost about ten pounds in the course of the 1999 season, so the new muscle brought him to 203 pounds. He worked his entire body, focusing on increasing his strength while maintaining his flexibility. He wanted to build up the stamina he would need for the long season ahead.

Jeter's new muscles didn't just mean he could hit the ball farther; they also gave him the ability to swing the bat faster. More bat speed meant that he could wait longer before swinging, which made him a better judge of how a pitch is moving.

The Yanks started off the 2000 season hoping to put together another spectacular year. They wanted to win their third World Championship in a row.

Jeter went 5 for 32 at the plate in April. Then, while taking extra batting practice, he suffered an abdominal strain. As a result, he spent part of May on the disabled list. Jeter watched from the sidelines in frustration as his teammates battled their way through the next twelve games. When he recovered, he was placed in the lineup against the Red Sox, where he immediately took charge. He went 3 for 4, logging three hits in four at bats along with stealing a base and scoring a run. The Yankees won 8–3.

By the All-Star break in July, the Yankees had compiled a solid record of 45–38. Jeter wanted to make sure he helped his team pick up the momentum it needed in the second half of the season to make it back to the World Series once again. But in the meantime, he had a chance to steal a bit of the All-Star spotlight.

Chapter Seven

MVP

In 2000 Derek was chosen to take part in the All-Star game for the third year in a row. Originally Alex Rodriguez—the top vote getter yet again—was slotted to start the game at short. But when A-Rod suffered a concussion in early July, Jeter was promoted to starting shortstop.

In both of Derek's prior All-Star at bats, he'd struck out. But he didn't dwell on his past performances. He told the press he applied the same strategy to the All-Star game that he did to his regular-season matchups. "I basically had the same game plan against everyone," he said. "I'm a free swinger."

On this night, Jeter's approach worked brilliantly. No matter where he swung, he always seemed to connect with the ball. In the first inning, he doubled off pitcher Randy Johnson for the AL's first extra base hit in two years of All-Star action. In the third, he singled and scored a run.

Even as a youngster, Derek Jeter dreamed of playing in the big leagues.

Derek hit better than .500 in his junior and senior years of high school.

Classmates.com Yearbook Archives

The Greensboro Bats

Jeter played minor league ball with the Class A Greensboro Hornets in 1992 and 1993.

After he joined the New York Yankees, Jeter impressed fans with his athletic abilities at shortstop.

In a 2000 parade celebrating the Yankees' third-straight World Series victory, Jeter records the excitement around him. Second baseman Chuck Knoblauch *(right)* is next to him.

Jeter's Turn 2 Foundation encourages kids to stay drug- and alcohol-free.

Derek's father, Charles Jeter *(left)*, is a substance abuse counselor who runs the Turn 2 Foundation.

Jeter dashes toward home plate and his cheering teammates after slamming the game-winning home run in game four of the 2001 World Series.

Alex Rodriguez *(left)* and Derek Jeter were rival shortstops, but they became teammates in 2004 when Rodriguez signed on as the Yankees' new third baseman.

Jeter displays his speedy baserunning in the 2004 American League Division Championship series against the Boston Red Sox.

And when Jeter faced Al Leiter in the fourth inning, the confident Yankee swung at the first pitch, hitting the ball into center field and driving in two runs.

The AL won the game 6–3, and at the end, Jeter was awarded the game's Most Valuable Player (MVP) trophy. Much to Jeter's surprise, he learned that this was the first time a Yankee had ever won that prize. To commemorate the occasion, the bat Jeter used that night was sent to the National Baseball Hall of Fame in Cooperstown, New York.

❝In due time, when I sit down and get a chance to reflect on it, then you realize how special it is. And I wasn't aware that no Yankee, no other Yankee, had won this award, and it's kind of hard to believe.❞

—DEREK JETER ON BEING THE FIRST YANKEE TO WIN THE ALL-STAR MOST VALUABLE PLAYER AWARD

The entire Yankee squad seemed energized after the All-Star break. They went on a home-run rampage, slamming fifty-three homers in thirty-four games. Jeter contributed with a two-run homer of his own in late July.

By mid-September, the Yanks led their division by six games, but the team seemed to lose focus. On September 19, the Bronx Bombers lost to the Toronto Blue Jays 16–3. Afterward

Jeter said, "We're playing terrible, and that's the bottom line. We're not hitting, we're not pitching, we're not playing defense." The team ended the month by losing seven games in a row. Jeter tried to rally his teammates' spirits, batting .548 in the final weeks of the season. The Yankees did have one lucky break—they still managed to clinch the division title because the second-place Red Sox weren't winning either.

BERNIE WILLIAMS

Bernabe Figueroa Williams grew up playing baseball in Puerto Rico. He joined the major leagues in 1991 with the Yankees and has become an essential member of the team. The center fielder is a four-time Gold Glove winner, and his abilities as a switch-hitter make him a powerful threat at the plate.

At the end of the regular season, Jeter's stats looked great. He had a .339 batting average with fifteen homers and seventy-three RBIs. Along with teammate Bernie Williams, Jeter distinguished himself by going five straight seasons with more than one hundred hits—including his 1,000th career hit during a 3–4 win against Detroit in September.

The Yankees faced the Oakland A's in the ALDS, and based on the Yankees' recent record, many declared them the underdogs. When the Yankees lost the first game, it only seemed to confirm that they were struggling. But then Torre mixed up the lineup, with Jeter batting leadoff, and the team won games two and three. Oakland was shut out in game two and only managed to score two runs in game three. With such a weak offense, they no longer looked like such a threat. Even so, the Yankees seemed a little *too* relaxed in game four. The Yanks lost that game 11–1, but they refused to give up. They scored six runs in the first inning of game five, eventually winning 7–5 to take the series.

When the Yankees met up with the Seattle Mariners for the ALCS, Jeter found himself pitted against his good friend Alex Rodriguez. He and Rodriguez both assured reporters that their friendship off the field wouldn't diminish their competitive drive on the field. "We're close," admitted Jeter, "but [A-Rod] knows I want to beat his team as much as any other team."

In game one, the battle between the two shortstops didn't go well for Jeter—he struck out three times while A-Rod hit a home run to lead his team to a 2–0 win. In game two, however, the situation was reversed—Jeter hit a two-run homer in the eighth inning to help the Yankees to a come-from-behind win. The Yankees surged ahead in the series, winning games three and four, with Jeter hitting a three-run homer in game four. The Mariners took game five in Seattle, but then the series moved back to Yankee Stadium. The Yankees fell behind 4–3 in game six, but they rallied in the seventh inning with six runs. The Mariners scored three more in the eighth, but the Yankees held them off after that point. The Yankees won the game 9–7 in front of a jubilant home crowd.

❝ *They don't get rattled over there. They play their game. You've got to give them credit for what they've been able to achieve. It's something that really doesn't happen in sports too often anymore. When that game starts, you've got to go out and beat them.* **❞**

—SEATTLE MARINERS MANAGER LOU PINIELLA, AFTER THE 2000 ALCS

During the playoffs, the Yankees had some surprising new supporters. New York's Mets fans were rooting enthusiastically for the "boys in pinstripes." Although the Mets play in the NL and the Yanks are in the AL, New Yorkers have always chosen to support only one of their town's two teams. This year something was different—the Mets had finished second in their division but clinched the wild-card spot and won the NLCS for the first time since 1986. New Yorkers of all stripes wanted to see a "Subway Series."

A Subway Series pits two New York City baseball teams against each other and fans can literally take the subway to all the games. The last Subway Series had taken place in 1956, when the Yankees beat the Brooklyn Dodgers. "It's hard enough for one [New York] team to make it," Derek explained. "But it's out of the ordinary for both of them."

In 1958 the Dodgers and the New York Giants both relocated to California. New York went four years without a second major league team until the Mets began playing in 1962. The Mets' team colors are blue and orange, combining Dodger blue with Giant orange.

Although most baseball experts agreed that the Mets were vastly overmatched in the series, the passion of their fans had pushed the team further than anyone had expected. The excitement of finally competing in their first Subway Series—and the thought of actually defeating the fabled Yankees—spurred on the players.

The series opened at Yankee Stadium, and the Yankees took the first game 4–3. It wasn't an easy win, though: The game dragged on for twelve innings. Jeter's big moment came in the sixth inning, when he made a great throw to home, preventing

Mets outfielder Timo Perez from scoring. In game two, Jeter doubled in the eighth inning and scored the run that would be the deciding factor in the Yankees' 6–5 win. The Mets responded by taking game three at Shea Stadium.

GAME ONE

At four hours, fifty-one minutes, game one of the 2000 World Series was the longest game in series history. It actually ended at 1:04 the morning of October 21. When it was finished, the Mets had gone through six pitchers and the Yankees had used four.

Jeter led off game four, facing Mets pitcher Bobby J. Jones. On the very first pitch, Jeter cracked the ball into the left-field bleachers. He was only the eighth player in history to lead off a World Series game with a home run. "I got a good pitch to hit," he said afterward, trying to downplay his achievement. "Fortunately, it carried out."

In the third inning, Jeter whacked a triple to right-center field. Luis Sojo's ground ball allowed Jeter to score, and the Yankees went on to win 3–2. The Yankees were one game away from their third-straight World Championship.

Second Base Switch

During the 1999 and 2000 seasons, Chuck Knoblauch began struggling at second base, consistently making throwing errors. He remained strong at the plate, so Torre often used him as the team's designated hitter. Luis Sojo began filling in at second base. Sojo had a knack for performing well when the team was under pressure.

After five innings of game five, the Mets led 2–1. But when Jeter came to bat in the top of the sixth, he slammed an Al Leiter fastball to far-left field for a game-tying homer. The game remained tied until the top of the ninth, when the Yanks squeezed out two more runs. In the bottom of the inning, with two outs, Mets slugger Mike Piazza stepped up and smacked a ball to deep center field. But Bernie Williams made the catch, and the game was over. The Yankees were World Champions for the third year in a row! No other team had pulled off three straight World Series wins since the Oakland A's had done it twenty-six years earlier.

Jeter had only praise for the Mets after the game. "This is by far the best team we've played," he said. "All the games could've gone either way. Every year is a different story, but I'd be lying if I said this wasn't more gratifying. Oakland was the hottest team when we played 'em, Seattle was tough, and the Mets were the best team I've seen in five years."

CHANGING TIMES

During the 1956 Subway Series, a ride on the New York City subway cost 15 cents and a box seat at the game cost $5. By 2000 the price of a subway fare had risen to $1.50 and anyone wanting a box seat had to shell out a whopping $160. Player salaries changed even more dramatically in those forty-four years: The average annual salary for a major leaguer went from about $15,000 to $2 million!

Jeter managed to hit the ball safely in nine of his twenty-two turns at bat in the Subway Series—belting two home runs, two doubles, and one triple. He also walked three times and set a new record for crossing nineteen total bases in a five-game World Series. His batting average for the 2000 Fall Classic was an amazing .409.

"This kid right now—the tougher the situation, the more fire gets in his eyes," said Torre. "You don't teach that. It's something you have to be born with."

> *Huge at-bat, huge hit . . . He's Derek Jeter, man. That's what he's supposed to do.*
>
> —TEAMMATE PAUL O'NEILL

In the sixty-one postseason games he'd played in his career, Jeter had reached base safely in fifty-six contests. He also ended 2000 with a fourteen-game hitting streak in World Series matchups. When the final game of 2000 was over, Jeter was honored as the World Series MVP. He was the first player ever to earn All-Star MVP and World Series MVP honors in the same season. "This guy's incredible," said Yankee pitcher Mike Stanton. "I don't think there's any doubt. He's the leader of this team."

Jeter was ecstatic about his team's success. But even after four World Series wins in five years, he had no plans to take it easy. He planned to spend the winter training hard, hoping for a shot at a fourth-straight championship title.

Chapter Eight

Celebrity

In spite of the awards he'd received in 2000, Derek approached the 2001 season with thoughts of improving his game. "I can always get better," he explained.

His teammates continued to speak highly of him. "There's no doubt New York is the capital of the baseball world . . . and Derek Jeter is its shining star," pitcher David Cone raved. Derek appeared in ads for a sports drink and a bank. He even starred in a Nike commercial with basketball icon Michael Jordan. Joe Torre claimed that the demand for Jeter went beyond his boyish good looks and baseball ability, saying, "There's something about his presence that makes you feel good."

When he wasn't playing, Jeter spent time in the community, talking to his supporters about life choices. As a baseball prospect, Jeter had watched a number of older players use chewing tobacco. He spoke out against the practice, emphasizing that it could cause cancer. "I think it's a nasty habit," Jeter said. "I've never used it. It's bad for you, but it's not the most appealing sight either."

Jeter continued to expand the Turn 2 Foundation, working to convince youngsters to stay away from drugs and alcohol. And he started working with the Jackie Robinson Foundation to help provide college scholarships for minority youngsters.

JACKIE ROBINSON

Jackie Robinson was the first person at the University of California at Los Angeles to letter in four sports—baseball, basketball, track, and football. This gifted athlete became the first African American to play major league baseball when he joined the Brooklyn Dodgers in 1947. He won the first-ever Rookie of the Year Award that year, and two years later he was named NL MVP.

Even with everything Jeter did—on and off the field—he tried to lead a balanced life. After six years in the major leagues, he'd become an expert at pacing himself between games. "The road is the best place to catch up on your rest," he reported, "because there are less demands on your time than there are at home."

He often began a day on the road by ordering breakfast in his hotel room, taking a nap, eating lunch, and then leaving for the ballpark. "I do it again the next day," he said. "I'm a creature of habit, so I eat at the same restaurants. I have places in every city that I go, and that's that."

OFF-SEASON SCARE

Not long after the 2000 World Series, doctors diagnosed Sharlee Jeter with Hodgkin's disease, a type of cancer. She underwent treatment during the off-season, and by the spring she was declared cancer-free.

Jeter spent much of the off-season in Florida as usual, this year focusing on his defensive skills. Meanwhile, reporters focused on his negotiations for a new contract with the Yankees. In December 2001, Alex Rodriguez inked a $252-million, ten-year deal with the Texas Rangers, setting a new salary record. Baseball observers debated whether Jeter might be worth even more money than his friend. In the end, Jeter settled for the second-highest contract in sports history, $189 million over ten years. Best of all for Jeter, the agreement in essence guaranteed that he'd remain a New York Yankee for his entire major league career.

> 66*It's always been my dream to play for the Yankees,
> and now I know this dream can last.*99
>
> —DEREK JETER, AFTER SIGNING
> A TEN-YEAR CONTRACT WITH THE YANKEES

Jeter missed the 2001 season opener after he had trouble with a sore throwing shoulder followed by a strained quadriceps (thigh) muscle. He sat out only a few games, but his April stats weren't his best: .289 with two home runs, seventeen RBIs, and seven errors. Jeter turned things around in a May game against the Red Sox when he went five for five with one home run—his first five-hit game in the majors.

Jeter found a new double-play partner that year in Alfonso Soriano. Soriano had been born in the Dominican Republic, and he spent three seasons playing baseball in Japan, where he learned to speak fluent Japanese and caught the attention of Yankee scouts. Although he'd been a shortstop in Japan, the Yankees obviously had that position covered. Soriano began spring training in left field, but when Knoblauch's throwing problems recurred, Soriano and Knoblauch switched positions.

The Yankees spent May and June battling the Red Sox for first place in the division. The team looked strong at the All-Star break, and Jeter's teammates wished him luck in his fourth

All-Star appearance. In the sixth inning, Jeter blasted his first-ever All-Star home run. Next up was Magglio Ordonez of the White Sox, who came to bat and did the exact same thing. It was the fifth time that back-to-back home runs ever occurred in an All-Star game. And it was the first time a Yankee had hit a homer in the midseason matchup since Yogi Berra did it in 1959.

2001 ALL-STAR GAME

The 2001 Midsummer Classic was especially meaningful for one of Jeter's heroes, Baltimore Oriole shortstop Cal Ripken Jr. Ripkin had spent twenty-one years in the major leagues, and he was about to retire. As he came to bat in the third inning, the crowd rose in a standing ovation. Ripkin stepped away from home plate and tipped his batting helmet to the cheering fans. Then he turned around and drilled a home run.

As in the past, Derek heard others compare him to Joe DiMaggio and Mickey Mantle. And once again, Jeter replied that it was too early to make those types of associations. "I think that's a huge compliment," he said. "But it's something I don't really think much about. That's judged when your career is over."

On July 13, Jeter had one of the worst games of his major league career—he fumbled several balls in the field and hit a groundout, a line out, struck out, and then hit into a double play. The Yankees had a rough August, but they started off strong in September.

In 2001 Jeter was chosen to host the comedy show *Saturday Night Live*. Guests on this program perform live. If something went wrong in the course of the night, Derek would have to improvise. "I'm still a little scared," he said several days before the broadcast.

Then on September 11, 2001, the world forgot about baseball. A group of hijackers took over four airplanes and attacked the World Trade Center in New York City and the Pentagon in Washington, D.C. Major League Baseball put its schedule on hold. The tragedy hit especially close to home for Jeter and his teammates, some of whom had apartments only a few miles from the twin towers. The players took several days off to spend time with family and friends.

Play finally resumed on September 17. The Yankees had their first game on September 18, against the White Sox in Chicago. The Yankees won 11–3. The following night in Chicago, Jeter slammed two home runs for his first multiple-homer game since 1998.

Although White Sox fans typically enjoyed jeering the Bronx Bombers, some people held up signs that read, "I Love NY." As the Yankees traveled to stadiums around the country, they were cheered by opposing fans who wanted to show their support for all New Yorkers.

The Yanks finished the season in first place in the AL East. But they went into the postseason with a lot of injured players—including starting pitchers Orlando "El Duque" Hernandez and Andy Pettitte and ace reliever Mariano Rivera. The team lost games one and two of the ALDS to the Oakland Athletics in Yankee Stadium. One more loss and the Yankees would be out for the season. In his six years with the Yankees, Jeter had never been in this situation. But the young star was confident. "We always do well when we have our backs to the wall," he told reporters.

Jeter was true to his word. In the seventh inning of game three, the Yankees were ahead 1–0. With two outs and Jeremy Giambi on first base, Oakland's Terrence Long doubled to the right-field corner. Giambi took off, rounding second and third and barreling toward home plate with the tying run. Right fielder Shane Spencer launched the ball toward the infield, but his aim was off and the ball missed both cutoff men. Out of nowhere, Jeter raced toward the first-base foul line, grabbed the ball on a bounce, and made a sidearm flip to catcher Jorge Posada. Posada snared the ball and tagged the back of Giambi's leg just as he reached the plate. The home plate umpire called Giambi out, and the Yankees went on to win the game.

THE LIFE YOU IMAGINE

Jeter came out with a book titled *The Life You Imagine: Life Lessons for Achieving Your Dreams,* in 2001. He hoped the book would reach young people who didn't have the chance to become involved with the Turn 2 Foundation. "Everyone needs a little encouragement," he wrote. "I hope my story will help inspire you to chase your dreams."

The Yankees charged through game four with a 9–2 win. Early in game five, Jeter hit a long fly ball, scoring Knoblauch and giving the Yankees a 4–2 advantage. A few innings later, he chased down a Terrence Long foul pop-up hit to left field, leaping into the stands and taking a hard fall to make the out. The

Yanks won the game 5–3. With a series batting average of .444, Jeter was named ALDS MVP. "I guess that's the reason he's wearing so many [World Series] rings," remarked Oakland manager Art Howe. "Whenever they need a big play, he's there to make it. Whenever they need a big hit, he gets it."

The Yankees then took on the Seattle Mariners in the ALCS. The Mariners were coming off one of the best regular seasons in major league history, with a record of 116–46. The Bronx Bombers refused to be intimidated. They defeated Seattle four games to one to win the ALCS. But Jeter struggled at the plate, hitting .118. Although he wouldn't discuss it, some suspected that he had lingering pain and stiffness from his acrobatic catch in game five of the ALDS. Ever the team player, Jeter wasn't about to sit out a game because of injuries that he considered minor; he had played every inning of every postseason game since 1996. He didn't want to let his team down.

Chapter Nine

Mr. November

In the 2001 World Series, the Yankees squared off against the Arizona Diamondbacks, a team that had only been playing since 1998. The Diamondbacks' past few seasons had been strong, and they'd just knocked out the Yankees' familiar World Series opponents, the Atlanta Braves, to win the NLCS. The Diamondbacks were led by two powerful pitchers, Curt Schilling and Randy Johnson.

The Yankees, however, had extensive World Series experience to draw on. Even though the team had never played in Phoenix's Bank One Ballpark, they appeared confident. Much to their shock, New York lost game one in Arizona, 9–1. Jeter went 0 for 3 but scored his team's only run after getting on base when Schilling drilled him in the wrist with a pitch. The Yankees expected to come back in game two, but they lost 4–0. The dominant Johnson struck out seven Yankees in the first three innings alone. But the Bronx Bombers returned to their home turf for game three, and starting pitcher Roger Clemens led them to a 2–1 victory.

Because of the events of September 11, the World Series had started later than it usually does. On October 31, when the baseball season is usually over, the Yankees and Diamondbacks began the fourth game of the Fall Classic. Thanks to pitching from Schiller and El Duque, neither team racked up many hits. But the Diamondbacks seemed to have an edge, and they led 3–1 after the top half of the ninth.

Clock Watching

Joe Torre's contract with the Yankees was scheduled to run out at midnight on October 31, 2001. During that game, Jeter teased Torre about how many minutes were left on his contract and asked him whether he would continue coaching the team after the clock struck twelve.

Arizona reliever Byung-Hyun Kim, a talented Korean establishing his name in American baseball, took the mound. Jeter bunted and was thrown out. Paul O'Neill managed a single, but then Bernie Williams struck out. With one out to go, first baseman Tino Martinez stepped up and slammed the ball straight back over the center-field wall for a two-run homer. The game went into extra innings. Arizona didn't score in the top of the tenth, and in the bottom half, neither Scott Brosius nor Soriano was able to get on base. At midnight—November 1—Derek Jeter stepped up to the plate.

"Welcome to November Baseball," flashed the scoreboard at Yankee Stadium. It was the first time a Major League Baseball game had ever been played in November.

Kim eyed Jeter and threw two strikes at him. Jeter fouled off the next two pitches and then took a ball. The count was one ball and two strikes. Jeter carefully watched the balls coming his way until the count was full. Finally Kim threw the pitch that Jeter wanted to see—a fastball. Jeter blasted it to right field. Reggie Sanders, the Diamondback right fielder, tried to catch it, but the ball was just too high. He stood, watching, as it arced into the bleachers.

❝When I first hit it, I had no idea whether it was going to go out, but once it goes out, it's a pretty special feeling. . . . I've never hit a walk-off home run before so it was a special experience.❞

—DEREK JETER

The fans in Yankee Stadium went wild. Jeter pumped his fist while rounding the bases. He was only the twelfth player in World Series history to end a game with a home run. When he reached home plate, he was mobbed by his overjoyed teammates. Reggie Jackson, the Yankees' old "Mr. October," was in the stands, applauding, as Derek was given a new nickname, "Mr. November."

Reggie Jackson

In 1977 Reggie Jackson signed with the Yankees for the highest salary in baseball at that time. He had a solid season, and when the World Series came around, he really kicked it up a notch. In game six, he clouted three home runs off three Los Angeles Dodgers pitchers. When the Yankees faced the Dodgers again in the 1978 World Series, Jackson smashed another home run. By the time the Yankees won the 1978 championship, Jackson had become the first player to hit seven homers in back-to-back World Series. Newspaper writers labeled him "Mr. October," and the nickname stuck.

The teams played another close game at Yankee Stadium the following night. Arizona scored two in the top of the fifth, and when the Yankees came up in the bottom of the ninth, they were still scoreless. And Kim was back on the mound. Posada hit a double, and then Kim quickly retired the next two Yankees. But the Bronx Bombers knew what to do. Third baseman Scott Brosius, who had not been having a strong series, stepped up and walloped Kim's second pitch into the left-field bleachers. The Yankees weren't out of it yet!

After a scoreless tenth, the Diamondbacks loaded the bases in the eleventh, but Alfonso Soriano made a diving catch to stop a line drive and prevented the runners from advancing. Chuck Knoblauch got on base in the twelfth inning, Brosius hit a sacrifice bunt to move him to second, and Soriano singled to send him home. He crossed the plate and leapt into the air. Jeter and the rest of the Yankees rushed from the dugout to congratulate Knoblauch and Soriano. The fans in Yankee Stadium roared even louder than they had the previous night. "This is the most incredible couple of games I've ever managed," said Torre.

With a 3–2 advantage, the Yankees returned to Arizona to finish off the series. But in game six everything fell apart—the Diamondbacks scored fifteen runs in the first four innings to rout the Yankees 15–2. Since the Yankees' streak of success had begun in 1996, the team hadn't played a seven-game World Series. They simply had never needed that many games to win.

Arizona pitcher Curt Schilling and Yankee pitcher Roger Clemens faced off for the final game, putting everything they had into every throw. The game remained scoreless until the Diamondbacks managed a run in the bottom of the sixth. The Yankees came right back in the seventh, with Jeter scoring on a Martinez single. Soriano led off the eighth inning with a home run, and it looked like another Yankee rally was under way. Mariano Rivera, the Yankees' unbeatable closer, stepped in to pitch the bottom of the eighth. He faced four batters and struck out three. New York didn't score in the top of the ninth, but their victory seemed all but certain.

Mariano Rivera was a key player in the Yankees' postseason dominance from 1998 through 2000. He hadn't had a postseason loss in 1,479 days—since game four of the 1997 ALDS.

And then Rivera faltered. Several Arizona players got on base, and Tony Womack hit a game-tying double. Rivera lost a little control and hit the next batter with a pitch, loading the bases. With Luis Gonzalez at bat, the infield moved forward. When batters managed to hit Rivera's pitches, they often could only manage dribbling grounders that didn't get much distance. But Gonzalez hit the ball up—a weak pop fly to shortstop. Jeter was too far forward to snag the ball, and the outfielders were too far back. The ball fell in the hole, and Arizona scored the winning run. The long, hard season was over. For the first time in four years, the Yankees weren't the World Series champions.

After the series, critics had a lot to say about the Yankees' weak offense. The team's batting average for the series was .183. Jeter had a paltry .148. In seven games, the Diamondbacks outscored the Yankees 37–14.

Yankee fans were disappointed, but not as much as they might have been at the end of an ordinary season. After September 11, no one felt quite normal yet. And New Yorkers were grateful to Jeter and his teammates for helping them forget their troubles for a while.

Chapter Ten

Captain

The 2002 season would be one of milestones for Derek. On opening day, Jeter banged out his 100th home run and 1,200th career hit during the Yankees' loss to the Baltimore Orioles. On April 19, while playing the Toronto Blue Jays, he collected his 500th career RBI. On June 10, he participated in his 1,000th major league game and managed to hit a home run against Arizona. On June 28, in an interleague contest against the Mets at Shea Stadium, he stole a career-high three bases. Jeter finished the season with respectable stats—a .297 average, 18 home runs, and 75 RBIs.

The Yankees played well in the regular season, and fans took it for granted that the Yankees would end up in the 2002 playoffs. And the Bronx Bombers didn't disappoint, defeating the Detroit Tigers on September 21 to win their fifth-straight division title. In the ALDS against the Anaheim Angels, Derek hit .500, logging his 100th postseason hit in the first inning of game four with a single off pitcher Jerrod Washburn. But the Angels were a scrappy, tight-knit team that year. They eliminated the Yankees in just four games en route to becoming World Series champions. It was the Yankees' earliest postseason exit since 1980.

A Good Guy

In 2002 *The Sporting News* named Jeter number one on its list of "The Good Guys" in professional sports for his ongoing success with the Turn 2 Foundation.

Jeter started off 2003 by dislocating his shoulder in the season opener. He dove headfirst into third base, colliding with Blue Jays catcher Ken Huckaby, who was covering third. Derek was forced to sit out thirty-six games before he could take the field again. Even without Jeter, the team was strong, winning twenty-five of those games. When Jeter rejoined the team in mid-May, he went on a thirteen-game hitting streak.

Through the Yankees' triumphs and disappointments, Derek had always been a loyal team member. Because he started his career in the lowest levels of the team's minor league system, he felt like he'd grown up with the Yankees. For the past several years, he'd been considered a team leader. In 2003 owner George Steinbrenner decided to reward the highly admired athlete by officially naming him team captain. In June "the Boss" made Jeter the Yankees' first captain since Don Mattingly had retired in 1995. Jeter didn't expect the new responsibility to cause any big changes, however. "[Steinbrenner] says he wants me to be a leader, like I have been," he told reporters. "The impression I got is to continue doing what I've been doing."

Jeter was only the eleventh captain in Yankee team history. In the past, the title had been held by, among others, Babe Ruth and Lou Gehrig. The news came as no surprise to Joe Torre, who commented, "When [Jeter] first came here, the other players seemed to gravitate toward him, so I thought this day would come eventually."

❝I feel honored to go watch him play. . . . He's one of those guys I wish I'd played long enough to play with. . . . That would have been fun.❞
—FORMER YANKEE CAPTAIN DON MATTINGLY ON DEREK JETER

At this point in his career, Derek was richer than he'd ever imagined, receiving an annual salary of more than $15 million— a $1 million raise from the year before. Because of his work ethic, he felt obligated to earn his paycheck every day. Still, in professional sports, injuries are inevitable, and Jeter was frustrated when he found himself on the disabled list in September 2003.

Jeter missed five matchups after straining a rib cage muscle. But when he was able to play, he maintained his All-Star-caliber abilities. Jeter ended the season with a .324 batting average, third in the league. He also had 10 home runs and 52 RBIs. The Yankees had a strong season, winning 101 games to finish first in the AL East for the sixth year in a row.

The Yankees met up with the Minnesota Twins in the first round of the playoffs. The Twins gave them a scare in game one, winning 3–1 in Yankee Stadium, but the Yanks won the next three in a row to take the series.

The Red Sox beat Oakland to square off against the Yankees in the ALCS. Baseball fans across the country took note, wondering if this was the year the Red Sox might break the Curse of the Bambino. Boston started well, winning game one, but New York came back to win games two and three. Boston won again in game four, and the Yanks split a pair of wins with the team in games five and six. Neither team was willing to yield any ground in game seven, and after nine innings the game was all tied up. In the bottom of the eleventh, Yankee third baseman Aaron Boone hit a ball out of the park to finish off the Red Sox 6–5.

The seasoned Yankees prepared to face a young Florida Marlins team in the 2003 World Series. The Marlins, like the Arizona Diamondbacks, were a recent addition to the major leagues. But unlike the Diamondbacks, the Marlins needed only six games to beat the Yankees. The series opened in New York, and the Yankees lost game one 3–2. It was the team's first World Series loss at Yankee Stadium since 1996. The Bronx Bombers fared better in games two and three, winning 6–1 each time. Game four went into extra innings, but Florida pulled off a 4–3 win. Yankees pitchers struggled in game five, and the team lost 6–4. Pitcher Josh Beckett mesmerized Yankee batters with his mix of curveballs, fastballs, and breaking balls. In game six, he pitched a shutout, and the Marlins won 2–0.

Jeter played well throughout the postseason, batting .314. He also set the record for career postseason hits with 123. But it was little consolation at the end of another imperfect season.

Steinbrenner didn't take losing well, and he vowed to do something dramatic to invigorate the lineup. He'd had his eye on Jeter's friend Alex Rodriguez, who belted forty-seven home runs for the Rangers in 2003. A-Rod won AL MVP honors, despite his team's fourth-place finish in the AL Central division. Of course, the Yankees already had one All-Star shortstop—what would they possibly do with two of them?

 In a single 2003 game, Rodriguez registered five hits against the Yankees.

In February 2004, a dapper-looking Alex Rodriguez strolled into a press conference at Yankee Stadium. Joe Torre announced that Rodriguez was joining the team as their new third baseman. The announcement made headlines nationwide, and Jeter realized that for the first time he'd be sharing the infield with a player who could possibly exceed him in popularity. But Jeter seemed perfectly at ease at the press conference as he helped A-Rod slip on Yankee pinstripes over a shirt and tie.

Jeter's 2004 season began with a nasty hitting slump, but he handled the setback with a mature attitude. Other players were known to slam their bats onto the ground after striking out and punch the dugout wall. But Derek refrained from throwing tantrums. "Everyone has bad days," he explained. "You have a bad day on the field, people sit and worry about it, it's over with. They can dwell on it all they want to. They can't change it. You strike out . . . you can throw your helmet, break a bat, do whatever you want. The bottom line is you still struck out."

Like Derek, Rodriguez is involved in charity work. He started the Alex Rodriguez Foundation in 1998, and he is one of three national spokespersons for the Boys & Girls Clubs. Through the organization, the player is overseeing the construction of an Alex Rodriguez Education Center near his south Florida home.

Even on his worst days, Jeter was aware of the fact that he'd get another chance to sparkle on the field. But when he went hitless in thirty-two at bats, the press began picking him apart. Was he no longer the player he'd been in the past? Was he intimidated by playing alongside A-Rod? Jeter answered every question patiently, never forgetting his role as team captain.

❝*I am Derek's biggest fan. When he does well, I am happy. He is as good a friend as I have in the whole world. I would give him the shirt off my back if he needed it.*❞

—ALEX RODRIGUEZ

Fellow Yankee Gary Sheffield noticed that when the Yankees were rallying, Jeter was always on the top step of the dugout, cheering on his teammates. "That's impressive," Sheffield commented. "I've seen a lot of guys in slumps before, and I've seen where they don't even come out and shake a guy's hand because they're so wrapped into themselves, they can't think straight. You would think Derek had four hits every night, the way he carried himself."

And the fans refused to give up on Jeter. When he came to bat at Yankee Stadium on April 29, the spectators stood and gave Jeter a standing ovation for good luck. Derek looked straight ahead at Oakland A's pitcher Barry Zito. Zito threw a fastball, and Jeter smashed it over the left-field wall and into Monument Park. The slump had ended with a home run. "It's like a bad dream is over with," Jeter said.

In June 2004, the Turn 2 Foundation held a fund-raising dinner in New York City. Jeter's guests included fellow Yankees

Bernie Williams, Hideki Matsui, and Kenny Lofton. More than five hundred people attended the event, called "Children Are Our Foundation . . . Teamwork Is How We Build It." By the end of the night, Jeter had raised $850,000 for kids in need.

With A-Rod at third base, Jeter won the balloting for the 2004 AL All-Star shortstop. He lived up to voters' expectations, going three for three. A few weeks after the season midpoint, Jeter had a seventeen-game hitting streak, tying the longest streak of his career. The Yankees continued to dominate their division, finishing in first with a 101–61 record. In more than half of the wins, the Yankees had come from behind. They also set a team record with 242 home runs. Jeter was only one homer away from tying his career high of twenty-four. He had a good year with a .292 average, 78 RBIs, and only 13 errors in the field.

The boys in pinstripes found themselves on familiar ground in the ALDS against the Minnesota Twins. The series was a virtual replay of 2003, with Minnesota winning game one at Yankee Stadium and the Yankees coming back to take the next three. As always, Jeter was a key player for the Yanks. He began game two with a leadoff home run, and later he scored the winning run. In game three, he drove in three runs. Jorge Posada praised him, saying, "He's a guy we follow. . . . He does it over and over again, and it's fun to see the way he approaches the game."

To add to the sense of déjà vu, the Yankees next played the Boston Red Sox for the division championship. New York was hoping for a shorter series this time around, and the team swept the first three games of the series. The Yanks won game three 19–8, and they looked unstoppable. No team had ever blown a three-game lead to lose a seven-game postseason series.

LONG BALL

Game four of the 2004 ALCS lasted twelve innings and was the longest major league postseason game ever at five hours, two minutes. But the record didn't last long. The very next night the Yankees and the Red Sox dragged out a fourteen-inning, five-hour, forty-nine-minute endurance contest.

But the Red Sox had made up their minds to throw off the Curse of the Bambino once and for all. Incredibly, they won games four and five in extra innings and then picked up even more momentum. They won the next two in nine innings, ending the Yankees' season earlier than expected. Boston went on to steamroll the St. Louis Cardinals, winning the team's first World Series in eighty-six years.

Jeter was shocked at the outcome. "Really, I never thought this would happen," he declared. "We had so much confidence going in, but were never overconfident. We never took things for granted. It just got away from us. I can't explain it." The team's offense had held up well during the playoffs, and Torre blamed a weak pitching staff for the team's early exit from the postseason.

No one was surprised to learn that Jeter's plans for the off-season included plenty of training in Tampa. Whatever the future holds, he'll continue playing his heart out for the Yankees. And once again he'll lead the charge for another World Series ring.

Future Hall of Famer

On June 26, 2004, Derek Jeter turned thirty years old. He was a different player than the kid first called up from the minor leagues in 1995, but he was just as promising. The day after his birthday, he hit two home runs in a game against the Mets. At the end of the 2004 season, Jeter's career batting average was .315, putting him in fifth place on the Yankees' all-time list of career averages.

Jeter and the Yankees welcomed another superstar to the team as they prepared for the 2005 baseball season. Sixteen-year veteran pitcher Randy Johnson joined the Yankees from the Arizona Diamondbacks.

But even on a team of superstars, Jeter remains a fan favorite and a true leader. He looked as strong as ever in spring training, racking up a .365 average in seventeen pre-season games.

The Yankees began the 2005 season playing a three-game series against the world champion Red Sox. The Bronx Bombers confidently won the first game 9–2, with Johnson pitching. The second game was close, and at the bottom of the ninth inning, the score was 3–3. Jeter led off and, on a 3–2 count, he blasted a home run to right-center field. It was the second walk-off homer of his career. The curse of the Bambino might be broken, but Jeter wasn't about to let that slow him down.

Alex Rodriguez has predicted that when Jeter's career is over, he'll be a sure thing for the National Baseball Hall of Fame. "I told him that I always thought he was a great player, but now that I am playing with him," A-Rod commented, "[I see] he is a greater player."

But Derek has years to go before he would even consider retirement. And if he is one day inducted into the Hall of Fame, he says he'll owe much of the credit to his teammates. "Personal accolades are great," he stated, "but you leave your place in history by playing on great teams."

Jeter's other plans for the future include marriage and a family. Although he has dated a number of famous women, he hasn't indicated whether he has a lucky lady in mind. "I wish to have a family soon," he admitted. "I'm not saying I'm in a rush but, yeah, that's definitely something I'll look forward to."

In life and in baseball, Jeter seems to know exactly what he wants. He's a star player, and he surrounds himself with wonderful family and friends. He understands that he might not ever have become a celebrity if he hadn't been willing to work hard for his goals. It's a philosophy that he hopes other young people will follow—whatever their ambitions may be. "I know what I want to do, and what I have to do," he emphasized. "I won't let anyone or anything get in the way of my goals."

PERSONAL STATISTICS

Name:

Derek Sanderson Jeter

Nicknames:

D.J., Mr. November

Born:

June 26, 1974

Height:

6'3"

Weight:

195 lbs.

Bats:

Right

Throws:

Right

BATTING STATISTICS

Year	Team	Avg	G	AB	Runs	Hits	2B	3B	HR	RBI	SB
1995	NYY	.250	15	48	5	12	4	1	0	7	0
1996	NYY	.314	157	582	104	183	25	6	10	78	14
1997	NYY	.291	159	654	116	190	31	7	10	70	23
1998	NYY	.324	149	626	127	203	25	8	19	84	30
1999	NYY	.349	158	627	134	219	37	9	24	102	19
2000	NYY	.339	148	593	119	201	31	4	15	73	22
2001	NYY	.311	150	614	110	191	35	3	21	74	27
2002	NYY	.297	157	644	124	191	26	0	18	75	32
2003	NYY	.324	119	482	87	156	25	3	10	52	11
2004	NYY	.292	154	643	111	188	44	1	23	78	23
	Total	.315	1,366	5,513	1,037	1,734	283	42	150	693	201

Key: **Avg**: batting average; **G**: games; **AB**: at bats; **2B**: doubles; **3B**: triples; **HR**: home runs; **RBI**: runs batted in; **SB**: stolen bases

FIELDING STATISTICS

Year	Team	Pos	G	C	PO	A	E	DP	FLD%
1995	NYY	SS	15	53	17	34	2	7	.973
1996	NYY	SS	157	710	244	444	22	83	.969
1997	NYY	SS	159	719	244	457	18	87	.975
1998	NYY	SS	148	625	223	393	9	82	.986
1999	NYY	SS	158	635	230	391	14	87	.978
2000	NYY	SS	148	609	236	349	24	77	.961
2001	NYY	SS	150	570	211	344	15	68	.974
2002	NYY	SS	156	600	219	367	14	69	.977
		DH	1	-	-	-	-	-	-
2003	NYY	SS	118	444	160	271	14	51	.969
2004	NYY	SS	154	678	273	392	13	96	.981
	Total		1,363	5,643	2,057	3,442	145	707	.974

Key: Pos: position; G: games; C: chances (balls hit to a position); PO: putouts; A: assists; E: errors; DP: double plays; FLD%: fielding percentage

BIBLIOGRAPHY

January, Brendan. *Derek Jeter: Shortstop Sensation.* New York: Children's Press, 2000.

Jeter, Derek, with Jack Curry. *The Life You Imagine: Life Lessons for Achieving Your Dreams.* New York: Crown Publishers, 2000.

Olney, Buster. *The Last Night of the Yankee Dynasty: The Game, the Team, and the Cost of Greatness.* New York: Ecco, 2004.

Schnakenberg, Bob. *Derek Jeter: Surefire Shortstop.* Minneapolis: Lerner Publications Company, 1999.

Thornley, Stew. *Alex Rodriguez: Slugging Shortstop.* Minneapolis: Lerner Publications Company, 1998.

WEB SITES

Alex Rodriguez and Derek Jeter Press Page

http://groups.msn.com/AlexRodriguezandDerekJeterPressPage

This site features an extensive archive of newspaper and magazine articles about these two players, dating to 1993.

New York Yankees: The Official Site

www.yankees.com

The official Yankees site has a ton of information, including career highlights for Jeter's years in the minor leagues and the major leagues.

Turn 2 Foundation

www.turn2foundation.org

The Web page for Derek Jeter's foundation provides a history of Turn 2, facts about the organization's many projects, and a few fun games.

INDEX